the little black book of

dating ideas

a buzz boxx book

John Graham / Stuart Ough / Morgan Taylor

Andrews and McMeel
A Universal Press Syndicate Company
Kansas City

ISBN 0-8362-2193-1

Library of Congress Catalog Card Number: 96-84533

ATTENTION: SCHOOLS AND BUSINESSES
Andrews and McMeel books are available at quantity discounts with bulk purchase for educational, business, or sales promotional use. For information, please write to: Special Sales Department, Andrews and McMeel, 4520 Main Street, Kansas City, Missouri 64111.

buzz boxx

Who are we?

the lost generation . . . slackers . . . generation x . . . whiners . . .
whatever. welcome to buzz boxx.

buzz boxx is a product company of, for, and about young people.
buzz boxx is made up of talented young people from various
backgrounds who create, make, and sell products intended for our
peers. sorry, no big 50-year-old v.p. of marketing trying to dictate
what we should like and buy. after all, we know what we like best.
it's a means for us to express ourselves in a positive way and bring
some smiles to people's faces. remember, life is way too short.
make a positive difference by what you do in the world around.

we're buzz boxx - the voice of young america

The buzz boxx team for this book includes:

John Graham— company mastermind
Stuart Ough—copy kat
Morgan Taylor—creative commissioner

Cover photos by Shannon McGlothin

Thanks to our "dating dilemma" friends who willingly mugged for the camera: Adria
G., David J., Debika C., Eric M., Jorge B., Katrina K., Kelley H., Kevin G., Kevin S.,
Lionel S., Madeline R., Mischa B., Mike B., Rob S., Samm L., and Todd T.

intro

This book's beginning is traced to a fateful panic attack brought on by the immense stress of last-minute planning for a first date.

Our story began as our mastermind sat on a crowded Chicago CTA bus heading home after a grueling day on the job. He found himself exasperated, struggling to think of any interesting ideas for that night's outing. You know the picture–tonight was a first date and he wanted desperately to think of something not so ordinary. After all, she could be special. So he sat, banging his head on the bus seat, wishing he had something to help in that grueling task, wishing he had some kind of easy reference guide to creative date ideas that went beyond dinner and a movie. Then life would be so simple, just close your eyes and pick.

Well, to make a long story not so long, he knew he wasn't alone, and that other people experienced this same dating dilemma and wished for a solution too.

So he teamed up with the rest of us who shared this same predicament. Together we've written a book's worth of creative dating ideas to make life a little easier, more fun, and, if you use this guide the way we hope you do, a little more memorable, too. And now, no more panic attacks.

Thanks and make it a great date.

buzz boxx

P.S. If you have other date ideas that you'd like to tell us about, we'd like to hear from you. We're already busy writing the next book. Turn to the last page for details.

What about something

simple &
easy

Write down your favorite items from this book and put them into a bowl. Or close your eyes and just point. Whatever you pick, do!

Mug for the camera. Pose together for some silly pictures in a photo booth.

Join forces. Adopt a street, sidewalk, or path in the woods that you can clean up on a regular basis.

Blow a few bucks at the video arcade. Play pinball.

Go to the airport to do some people-watching. Try to imagine where people are going. Watch the planes land and take off. Dream and talk about the places you'd like to go someday.

Play any sport together, like tennis or one-on-one basketball. Afterward, make some fruit smoothies to help cool down.

Build an enormous banana split for two.
Make pig noises as you chow down.

You're never too old to go antique shopping or to visit a used furniture store or flea market together.

Attend a convention together. Meet others who share an interest in *Star Trek*, Elvis, the Beatles, comic books, or cars.

Whisper sweet nothings into each other's ears. Go to Ben & Jerry's or Mrs. Field's cookies for a delicious snack.

Play dress up!

Indulge in your favorite snack foods and have a feast. Bring over all your favorite snacks like Hostess Ding Dongs, Ho Hos, Doritos, and Oreo cookies.

Take a ferry, river-, or paddleboat ride together.

Get to know each other better and reveal yourself.
Read *The Book of Questions* together.

Go for a drive in the countryside or into the city.
Throw out the map and explore the back roads.

Spend the evening telling each other
stories that have never happened to
you, but you wish had. They can be
as self-gratifying as possible.

Stay fit together. Join a gym. Work out or weight train together.

Don your fancy cowboy hats and boots and mosey on down to a country and western bar.

Idle the day away at an outdoor cafe and do some serious people-watching.

Read this book together.

Blow bubbles . . . anytime . . . anywhere.

Order in Chinese food. Eat with chopsticks.
Buy some cheap Chinese lanterns to create some ambience.
Don't forget the fortune cookies.

Spend Sunday reading the *New York Times* together.

Do you share a common interest and want to learn more? Take a class at a local community college, such as acting or photography, and see what develops.

Play racquetball.

Stay out all night searching for the best cup of coffee.

Visit a pet store and play with the animals.

On a beautiful day, lie on your backs and just watch the cloud formations roll by. Pick out shapes of animals, people, and scenes.

Attend a free concert. Many parks offer weekly concerts under the stars with free admission.

Make a breakfast date and go from there! Meet at a pancake house or waffle house. (This is only recommended if you're both *morning* people and don't suffer from gravitational hair shift during the night.)

Spend the entire date doing things you've
never done before.

Read chapters of a favorite book out loud. Take turns.

Why walk on eggshells? Break some instead and make an
omelette. Try something other than ham and cheese.

Get cultured. Visit an art museum.

Power walk. Talk as you walk and catch up on each other's lives.

Shop at a garage sale. Hunt for bargains and one-of-a-kind items.

Learn to cook together or learn how to cook your date's favorite food.

Shop at a farmer's market. Stroll through the stalls and look
for new or unusual produce you haven't tried.
Make something with it at home.

Cruise the strip, even if it's just for old times.

The sky's the limit. Visit a planetarium. Look for special
evening shows with interesting themes.

Go see a psychic and have your fortunes told for the fun of it.

Unwind at a coffeehouse. Try new coffees or teas. Relax and listen to poetry readings or chill out to the cool sounds of jazz.

Go sightseeing. Take a tour bus ride and get to know your city and its history better.

Saddle up and go horseback riding.

"Dating can be like a box of chocolates—you never know what you're gonna get." Buy a box of chocolates—the kind that you can't tell what's inside. Guess what's inside each piece before the two of you eat it.

Feed the ducks.

Join a bowling league together. This is great if you continue seeing each other or even if you don't. You can always take out your frustrations on the pins.

Study at home or the library.

Head to a local bar and challenge your
date to a game of darts. Make outrageous bets.

Watch the sunrise from a hilltop.

Go on a nature walk. Do some bird-watching.
Tune into the sights, sounds, and smells all around.

Play *mind* games with each other . . . like backgammon, chess, checkers, Chinese checkers, or Trivial Pursuit.

Attend a wedding together.

Look at family photo albums. It's a great way to learn about each other's family and friends.

Spend the day together helping someone else. Help friends move, your family clean, or any other kind gesture.

Do your laundry together at home or at the Laundromat.
(You may want to leave your dirty underwear at home
for this one.) Take lunch so you both can eat
while you clean.

Visit a natural history museum.

Do some window-shopping at a mall or downtown
after hours.

Learn to dance. Learn the latest hip-hop steps, line dances, or even how to ballroom dance.

Have a Blockbuster night. Rent a movie, microwave some popcorn, turn out the lights, and snuggle.

Go to church, then out to breakfast or brunch afterward.

Pack a lunch and go hiking or backpacking. Head for the hills, mountains, or woods for the day.

Visit a palm reader and have her read your hands.
How long are your love lines?

Make plans to watch a television miniseries and book your
date for each night of the show.

Watch a local high school sporting event.

Do a craft together; paint a picture or even paint by numbers.
Or share a hobby that you both can enjoy.

Take a sack lunch to a park bench and watch people. Guess or make up stories about them as they pass by.

Visit a children's museum with lots of interactive and participatory exhibits.

Play catch with a Frisbee.

Attend a school play.

Start with $10 each. Buy trinket gifts. See who can buy the most or funniest stuff for the other person. Meet back at a certain time and open gifts.

Play a round of miniature golf or set up your own indoor course using cans or plastic cups.

Go mountain biking and experience the fresh outdoors.

Concert tickets too expensive? Make your own concert in the backyard. Play compact discs of a favorite artist or group and listen on blankets.

Create a homemade pizza together. Use your favorite toppings or go crazy and try some different combinations, like pineapple and Canadian bacon, lobster and crabmeat, sausage and jalapeño peppers, or spinach and feta cheese.

Enjoy the usual—dinner and a movie.

Well, I have this idea that's really

different
& free

Spend the entire afternoon searching for the *best* elevator ride in your town. Try malls, hotels, and high-rise buildings.

Play bingo at a local church or community center. Use your winnings to pay for the next date or donate them to charity.

Watch an eclipse together, especially a lunar one.

Get away for the weekend, even if it's to your own backyard.
Camp out. Pitch a tent and sleep under the stars.

Volunteer together. Pick a soup kitchen or a homeless shelter.
Deliver food to AIDS patients or spend time with the elderly.
Work with younger kids. No matter what, you'll feel great
about the date.

Play "Follow the Leader" or "Simon Says." Take turns.

Feed each other while you're both lying on
your backs—head to head.

Play Twister and get tangled up together.

Make grilled cheese or peanut butter and jelly sandwiches
and serve them with chocolate milk. Share some of your
favorite childhood memories, like your best friends,
favorite toys, funny stories, favorite teachers, or
most embarrassing moments.

Listen to old music albums together. Guess songs by playing only a few notes. Reminisce about past favorite songs and memories associated with them.

Watch a sunset. Try to predict the next day's weather by looking at the colors in the sky.

Take a break from being all grown-up. Visit FAO Schwarz, Toys 'Я' Us or any toy store. Play with all the toys and games.

Pack a brown-bag lunch and watch a wrecking
ball demolish a building.

Visit a car dealership and test-drive cars.

Go to a bookstore. Pick out books that you think
the other person would like and read them together.

Jump on a trampoline.

Play spy! Try to hide from somebody you don't know or pick somebody on the street and try to follow them as closely as possible, for as long as possible, without being seen by them. When they are lost from sight, or you've been spotted, eat at the closest restaurant.

Ask one another about your dreams. Find a book on
how to interpret them. Help each other discover what they
really reveal.

Clean out a closet together. Have fun trying on old and
out-of-date clothes. Then donate your old duds to charity.

Go in-line skating or roller skating. Rent a pair of
Rollerblade skates and skate the day away.

Visit a state park. Take along a book on trees and identify different leaves.

Don't just walk through the park, climb a tree.

Do everything for the other person. Comb their hair, put their shoes on, open the door, drive them, take their coat, order the food, feed them . . . everything.

Spend the entire day getting as many free samples of things as you can, like food, fragrances, and more.

Bonjour. Learn a foreign language together. Check out language tapes from the library. Practice speaking it with each other. *Ciao.*

Ever feel tangled up? Do it for real and practice yoga together.

Take an architectural tour of your city or town. See who can spot the oldest building by finding and looking at the cornerstones.

Engage in a friendly pillow or food fight.

Visit your state capital building and watch government in action.

Make up silly and original *knock knock* jokes. For example: "Knock, knock. Who's there? Snew. Snew who? Snew that I'd have fun on this date."

Attend a lecture on a topic that you'd both enjoy. Share your thoughts later over an espresso.

Play on bales of hay.

Have a paper airplane fight or see who can throw theirs the farthest—very addictive!

Sing classic *bad* but very likable songs together: "We had joy, we had fun, we had seasons in the sun. . . ."

Explore the old town or ethnic parts of a city together.

Pick out the outfits you like best for each other and wear them on your date.

Meet each other at the perfume or fragrance counter of a major department store. Sample fragrances and select a *special scent* for each other.

Tell stories or make one up. Take turns adding a sentence or two to create your own continuous story line.
See where it goes.

Take a stand. Work on a political campaign or worthy cause together.

Join your local community theater and work together behind the scenes.

Hang out at the mall and play "find the person wearing _____ ." Keep score. Winner takes all.

Meet at a park playground and play. Swing each other, race down the slides, and bounce on the teeter totter. You're never too old to be a kid again.

Go to the library. Pick a favorite topic and find books to read together. Check out the foreign newspapers or listen to the many audiotapes.

Do a crossword puzzle.

Go on a pretend shopping spree. Imagine you have a million dollars to spend. Try on expensive clothes. Pick out clothes for each other!

I'm in the mood for something a little

romantic &
thoughtful

Rendezvous at midday on the rooftop of a building for a champagne toast, a gourmet snack, or even to sneak a kiss.

Read poems together or write one especially for your date. Try your hand at a love letter.

Take a sunrise bike ride. Show up unexpectedly with donuts and fresh orange juice.

Sing and dance in the rain. Splash in the puddles after a storm.

Agree to meet in a public place at a specific time. Pretend that you don't know each other and that you're meeting for the first time. Watch strangers as they eavesdrop on your conversation.

Surprise your date with breakfast in bed. Don't forget the rose.

Hire a friend to serve dinner for the two of you. Friends make excellent and inexpensive butlers and maids, as well as provide comic relief.

Create your own "like" pack filled with your date's favorite drink, candles, and music. Present it as a gift to set the right mood. Find out your date's favorite drink and music if you don't already know.

For anytime, turn off the lights and fill the room with candles.

What's cooking? Whip up a gourmet dinner together
or sign up for a gourmet cooking course.

Send a multiple-choice postcard or letter to ask
your date out.

On a clear night, drive to a remote spot, lie on top of your
car and watch for falling stars. Gaze at the stars and
constellations. Find the Big Dipper or try to spot satellites.
They're the ones that look like planes, but without
the blinking lights.

Splurge and take a carriage ride through the park or downtown.

Feed each other.

Take a walk in the moonlight.

Make a cassette tape of your favorite music, either together or as a gift for your date. Listen to it with each other.

For any romantic date, buy *the* dating essentials—flowers and a good bottle of champagne.

You don't always have to get together at night. Make a lunch date. Go someplace special. On a sunny day, eat at an outdoor cafe or a restaurant's garden patio.

On a clear night, pick out a star for one another and make them yours. Make and frame certificates for each other so it's "official." Wish on them when you're away from each other.

Relax in a hammock together and just swing.

Hire a friend to be your chauffeur for the evening.

Bake a batch of cookies together, even late at night.
Clean the bowl with your fingers.

On a hot summer's day, sit under a shady tree and take turns
reading poetry out loud while feeding each other juicy grapes
and strawberries.

Surprise your date at work or school
with a picnic lunch. Whisk your
date away with a basket full
of their favorite food and drink.

Hang white lights or Chinese lanterns inside or out to make any occasion special.

Give each other a massage—and don't forget the feet.

Do it in hot oil. Make fondue together. Start out dipping bread in melted cheese, then move on to meats, chicken, and vegetables cooked in hot oil, and finish off by scooping up melted chocolate with pound cake and fruits.

Turn off the lights and slow dance in the dark or by candlelight. Play a Frank Sinatra, Everything But The Girl, Luther Vandross, or Toni Braxton CD.

Spend hours tickling each other.

Surprise your date. Cook their favorite dinner.

View the planets, Moon, and stars through a telescope.

Say shocking or titillating things to each other
in a crowded elevator. Steal kisses
between floors.

Drive to the beach or lake. Take along a CD player and your
favorite songs. Dance under the stars and Moon.
The dance floor is all yours.

Go for a late-night swim. Float candles in the pool and place
luminarias around the patio for just the right touch.

While having dinner, hire someone to deliver flowers to your table.

On a cold night, lie down in front of a blazing fire with the lights off. Play soft music, cuddle under some blankets, enjoy a bottle of wine, and just hold one another.

Read *The Art of Kissing* out loud to each other and practice, practice, practice.

Playfully kidnap your date after school or work for a full evening of planned surprises, like a movie, carriage ride, and ice-skating.

Raid the refrigerator together. Take turns blindfolding and feeding each other. Guess what you're eating through smell, touch, and finally taste.

Stroll along a beach, river, or lakefront. Get your feet wet.

Meet at the piano bar of an expensive hotel for drinks.
Have a single rose delivered to your date by the
hotel bellman.

Locate and determine your favorite and *secret* meeting places
like a clock tower, flight of stairs, boardwalk, or graveyard.
Meet at a famous landmark or intersection if you like.
Make it your spot for heart-to-heart talks.

Rub a dub dub, go for a hot tub.

Plant a tree to celebrate a birthday, anniversary, or special occasion for the two of you.

Take a midnight, moonlit swim in the ocean, lake, river, or pool.

Have an Italian night at home. Play a Berlitz foreign language tape, serve pasta, play opera music, and watch a Fellini film. That's *amore!*

Meditate together with soft music and incense.

When the moon is full, take a midnight car ride and open the moon roof.

Dress in all-white vintage clothing and have a *classic* picnic on a hot, lazy afternoon.

Spend a clear afternoon at the
observation deck of a tall building,
such as the John Hancock Building
in Chicago or the Empire State
Building in New York City.
Or, have drinks at the top floor
of the tallest building in your area.
Go at night and let the city lights
mesmerize you.

Thou canst serenade thy date under their bedroom window
or balcony. (Or you can sing if you're not particularly
skilled in serenading.)

Try different restaurants. Make one your special place.

Take a tour of a winery and sample the wines afterward.
Take a wine tasting class beforehand.

Spend the evening spoiling your senses. Turn off the lights, burn scented candles, trade back rubs, and maybe indulge in a favorite, wicked dessert.

Feed each other with chopsticks.

Just hold each other.

Hey! Let's do something really

off the
wall

On a rainy day, have a picnic on your living room floor complete with paper plates, plastic ants, and an outdoor cassette tape from the Nature Company of a babbling brook or waves crashing against the shore.

Stay out all night discovering places that stay *open all night.*

Make up an alias for each other and pretend to be that person for the day in public.

Buy some balloons and create balloon animals, hats, or weird objects.

Pose as a news reporter from *Cosmopolitan*, *Rolling Stone*, *People*, *Details*, or any other cool magazine. Interview your date for real or for fantasy. Record the interview and take notes. Transcribe it later and add a picture. Present the written interview as a gift.

Go on an archeological dig.

Show up for your date dressed as a gorilla, a cocktail waitress, a nurse, a doctor, a professional athlete, or even a knight in shining armor.

Do something that you'll always remember—walk barefoot in the park for the fun of it on a cold winter's day, or jump into a public fountain with all your clothes on in the summer.

Have a pie fight with whipped cream.

Travel back in time to your senior year in high school. Decorate a room with streamers, set up a bowl of punch, dress in old formals, and dance to music from your graduating years. Or crash your old high school's prom and attend it again.

Dress in period costumes and attend a Renaissance festival together.

Be architects. Build a house or even a whole town using Lego building blocks. Build your dream house.

Find out more about your date by playing a game of hangman. Ask a personal question about your date and let the answer be revealed as part of the game.

Have tarot cards read for the two of you.

Go bowling. Make up your own rules. Roll the ball with your opposite hand. Close your eyes. Roll the ball between your legs. Push it with your foot. Do whatever.

Take a survival course together like Outward Bound,
self-defense, or CPR.

Learn how to milk a cow if you don't know how.
Make homemade ice cream.

Turn any dinner into a memorable occasion. Buy cheap
glasses and plates. Have fun throwing them into the fireplace
and breaking them after each course of the meal.

Write down on strips of paper the names of surrounding towns that you haven't visited. Put them into a bowl, draw one, and go explore.

Spend the evening communicating without words. Use your hands, eyes, and face. Act out words.

Make a date to watch Saturday morning cartoons together. Go all-out . . . eat Cap 'n Crunch cereal, wear your pajamas, and flip a coin to see who gets to keep the prize.

Steer off the beaten path. Blaze your own trails and
do a little 4x4 off-road muddin'. Yahoo!

When flowers just won't do, say it in stone. Buy cement mix.
Place your hands and feet in the cement to make prints.
Autograph and date it for true *Hollywood star* treatment.

Spend zee day talking wiz a foreign accent.
You can have zee best time wiz zis.

Have a "stick to the rules night."
Each person decides a secret set of
rules for themselves and must
adhere to them for the entire date.
For example, every time your date
picks up their fork, put yours down.
Let the rules become complex and
hide them as well as possible. Try to
figure out the other person's rules.

Make a movie together with a home video camera.
Borrow a friend's or rent one.

Buy temporary tattoos and paste them on each other's
arms, ankles, and shoulders.

Order 100 pounds of shaved ice and have
it delivered to your date's house or apartment.
Build a snowman . . . in the summer.

In the winter, import a beach and throw a beach party.
Fill a plastic pool with sand or water and turn up the heat.
Wear sunglasses, play Beach Boys music, put your feet in the
pool, and drink piña coladas.

Reenact your favorite scene from a movie or TV show that
you both love.

Visit a costume shop or theater department together.
Have fun trying on different outfits and costumes.

Dress up as mimes and go *clown* around the town
or in the park.

Record a song or even a music video together.

Announce that you are wearing one brand-new piece of
clothing that your date has never seen. Your date has to figure
out what it is, without questions, just observations throughout
the date. At the end, take a guess.
Right gets a treat, wrong . . .

Spend the entire day taking as many different modes of transportation as you can think of—a bus, the subway, a cable car, an elevator, an escalator, a taxi, a ferry, a . . .

Run through the sprinklers in a park, a neighbor's yard, or a golf course. Run through with all your clothes on.

Create a dream map. Cut out pictures from magazines and tell a story to your date about your hopes and dreams for the future.

Buy a guidebook for your city or town. Purchase matching outfits and be *tourists* for the day. Don't forget your cameras and maps. Ask strangers to take your picture.

Eat an entire meal without utensils. Use only your hands or no hands at all.

Change your image and fantasize about new hairstyles. Visit a mall or salon where you can pick a new "do" for each other on a computer.

Crash a wedding reception, convention, or dinner party.
Hey, it's free food.

Share your "stupid human tricks" with each other, like
balancing a spoon on your nose, making fangs with
your lips, levitating a pea with your mouth, wiggling
your ears, expanding your nostrils, or performing
famous celebrity impersonations.

Play with an Etch-A-Sketch.

Mooove over Bessie. Something you can only learn through trial and error—go cow-tipping at night. But be forewarned, not all cows sleep at the same time.

Make your way to a karaoke bar and sing a duet. If you're not ready for the public, rent a karaoke machine and pretend you're lounge acts.

Salvage an old chair or table at a used furniture store or junk yard. Fix it up and paint it together.

Relive the Summer of Love and be a flower child from the '60s. Watch the movie *Woodstock* or groove to the sound track. Paint flowers and peace signs on each other's faces. Dress like hippies.

Buy McDonald's Happy Meals. Play with the toys and do the activities and games on the boxes.

Improv to really bad movies. Turn off the sound on your TV or at the drive-in and make up your own dialogue together.

Go deer "hunting." On summer nights, tour the country roads
and use a strong flashlight to find deer in farmers' fields.
Have a contest to see who can spot the most.

Get a manicure together . . . and pedicure,
if you can *foot* the bill. (Stop us now!)

Build a tree house for the two of you. It can become
your secret getaway.

Practice scream therapy. Park near the train tracks
or airport runway. When a train goes by or
plane flies overhead, yell and scream at the
top of your lungs.

Send a *Mission Impossible*–like tape detailing where and
when to meet on your next date. Deliver it in an unusual
way. Or leave the message on your date's answering
machine.

For a bizarre twist on moviegoing, go to a movie blindfolded and listen to the crowd, or wear earplugs and watch their reactions.

Use sidewalk chalk that erases in the rain to draw pictures on the cement. Play tic-tac-toe or hopscotch, or write notes to each other.

Improvise the entire date. How do you use a chair? Stand on it or flip it on its side and sit on the edge. Act as if everything is normal though in fact it is not.

Watch '60s sitcoms on Nickelodeon and eat
frozenTV dinners.

Plan a treasure hunt. Be clever as you create clues to lead
your date to the hidden treasure.

Make up your own language. Spend the entire date
speaking a different language—one that doesn't exist.
Make up words as you go along and try to carry it through
the entire evening without faltering, even when
you order food.

Don't worry about it, I've got

money to
burn

Rent a limo and search for the *best* margarita in town.

Take a gamble and fly to Las Vegas for the weekend.

Go to a comedy club and laugh your heads off. Be sure to sit in the front row to get in on the act.

In one month, go through the alphabet and eat at a restaurant that begins with each letter.

Send a singing telegram to invite your date out.

Create your own "Best _____" list together. Have fun researching categories like best martinis, best music, best dessert, best crowd, best restaurant, and best romantic place.

Rent motorized vehicles for your dating pleasure like mopeds, jet skis, or motorcycles.

Eat Sunday brunch at an expensive hotel.

Put together a list of countries and their indigenous foods.
Learn how to cook these foods. Chart your progress on a map
as you eat and drink your way around the world.

Follow your favorite band or local group to nearby cities.

Go to an unglazed pottery shop where you can
paint cups, saucers, bowls, and other pieces together.
Pick them up after they've been fired. They make
great one-of-a-kind gifts.

Go to a concert. Expose yourself to new and different sights and sounds, such as attending the symphony, listening to a jazz or blues band, or seeing a ballet.

Bring over a catered dinner from your date's favorite restaurant.

Run away to the circus, even if it's just for the night. If Cirque Du Soleil is performing anywhere nearby, go. You won't regret it.

For real risk-takers and daredevils, go bungee-jumping, skydiving, hang gliding, white-water river rafting, rock climbing, or parasailing. But do it at your own risk.

Spend the day at the horse races. Make a bet to win, place, or show.

Visit a portrait studio. Have a costume portrait done. Dress in Civil War or Wild West clothing.

Be adventurous. Challenge your taste buds. Try new restaurants together. Try ones with ethnic foods that you've never had, like Russian, Caribbean, Greek, or Thai. Order food because you like the sound of the name.

Have your horoscope charts done together. A computerized service can give you your compatibility profiles, romance reports, and more.

Lasso your date and head to a rodeo.

Throw your own movie and film festival at home. Rent a marathon of movies that include your date's favorite actor, actress, director, or movie genre. This can be all-day fun!

Hire mariachis to serenade or play for you while having a Mexican dinner.

Have a progressive dinner date. Eat each course at a different restaurant. Have appetizers at one place, salad at another, entree at another, and dessert somewhere else.

Go on-line. As a couple, talk to somebody else on a bulletin board or chat room. Help each other with what to say. Take turns. Act as one person.

Look! Up in the sky! It's a bird! It's a plane! It's . . . you and your date? Go hot air ballooning or take a ride in a glider or helicopter.

Say cheese! Buy a disposable camera and spend the afternoon taking each other's pictures. Have a double set of photos printed at a one-hour photo lab.

Attend live theater or local plays. Buy season tickets.
At some places you can even volunteer to be ushers and see
the play for free.

For true spontaneity, go to the airport, buy the
cheapest flight to anywhere, and go do whatever.
And don't leave home without your
American Express card.

It's easy to come up with ideas when there's a

change of
seasons

Head to the slopes and go cross-country skiing, downhill skiing, tubing, or snowboarding.

After a good snow, build a snow family together or make snow angels.

Go ice-skating. Rent a pair of skates from a local sporting goods store and practice your triple toe loops and double axles.

Build snow forts and have a good old-fashioned
snowball fight.

Create your own holidays, complete with your own made-up
traditions. Celebrate a favorite actor or singer's birthday
together. Celebrate Picnic Day or First Day of
Spring over 60 Degrees Day.

Take time to stop and smell the roses . . . or tulips or lilies.
Visit a botanical garden and check out what's
blooming this time of year.

Dye Easter eggs together. Write secret messages on the eggs with a white crayon. Let the dye reveal them to your date.

Fly a kite on a windy day.

Have a birthday party.

Have a holiday photo taken together with Santa or the Easter Bunny.

Spend the afternoon on the water. Climb aboard
a sailboat or yacht.

Put your green thumbs together and plant a garden.
Try flowers, vegetables, herbs, or trees.

Whenever possible, have breakfast, lunch, or
dinner outdoors.

Attend local Shakespeare in the Park summer festivals.

Take the plunge and cool off on a hot summer's day at a
water park.

For a 10.0 date with a 3.5 degree of difficulty, go swimming
and diving at a public pool. Judge each other's dives off the
diving board or see who can make the biggest splash.
Cannonball!

Have a picnic at an arboretum, a park, a lake, a vacant
amphitheater, the beach, or the top of a high-rise
parking garage.

Feeling playful? Chase each other around with water soakers
or squirt guns.

Build sand castles in a sandbox or at the beach.

Catch some tasty waves. Go surfing, boogie-boarding,
water-skiing, jet-skiing, or windsurfing together.

Head to the beach and play volleyball. If there's not a beach around, make one in your yard by ordering some sand.

Oooh and aaah at the Fourth of July fireworks . . . and at each other, for that matter.

Float the day away. Go inner-tubing on a cool, lazy stream or share a raft.

Be a sport. Have a water balloon fight.

Celebrate Christmas in July or your favorite holiday every six
months. Celebrate Valentine's Day again on August 14th.

Sit on a porch together. Sip lemonade and listen to the
sounds of the evening. Catch fireflies.

Rake autumn leaves together in your yard or do it
as a favor for a neighbor.

Go to an orchard together and pick fruit like apples,
strawberries, raspberries, or blueberries.
Bake a pie afterward.

Drive to the country to watch autumn's show of changing
leaves. Drive to the highest point to see nature's reds,
oranges, and yellows over the horizon.

Don't let it pass you by. Attend a holiday parade or watch
one on TV during Thanksgiving or the holiday season.

Celebrate food at a festival. Attend a local festival or Oktoberfest.

Go for a hayride.

Go haunted-housing during Halloween or create your own for neighborhood kids.

Pick a pumpkin in the pumpkin patch. Carve jack-o'-lanterns. Roast and salt the seeds for a snack.

Decorate a Christmas tree together or host a tree-trimming
party. Play classic Christmas music like
Bing Crosby. Serve eggnog and
homemade cookies.

Enjoy Christmas decorations together. Drive around the
neighborhood to see everyone's decorations, or
downtown to see the store windows
and displays.

Sometimes I like dates that are

group
gatherings

Watch TV together. Make a date to watch a favorite weekly show like *Friends, Melrose Place,* or *Seinfeld.*

Organize an "Around the World" party. Each couple has a different country and makes food and drinks from that country.

Throw a painting party. Paint a room together. Paint a house if you're really ambitious. Order pizza or Chinese food and have it delivered.

Host a bad movie party together. Rent a bunch of bad movies. Serve movie theater–style popcorn and large drinks.

Create a theme party date and require costumes. Do a movie theme or murder mystery. Play music that fits the theme.

Wig out! Host a wig party where everyone wears a wig for the evening.

Have a barbecue at home, the beach, or a park. Grill some hot dogs, bring the badminton set, and crank up the music.

Rummage through your closet and pull out favorite childhood board games. Play Trouble, Mouse Trap, Battleship, or even the Game of Life.

Throw a real beer bash. Invite other couples over to sample beers from various microbrewers.

Invite friends over for a Cajun barbecue.
Cook up a big pot of jambalaya
complete with crawdads, or crayfish,
depending on what part of the country
you're from. Cover a long table with
plastic garbage bags. Serve the
jambalaya by pouring it down the
middle of the table. Give everyone
utensils and a cold beer and
have them pull up a chair.
Play creole or zydeco music.

Throw a cookout and swim party. Invite friends
or relatives . . . but as Mom always says, "wait 30 minutes
after eating before you get in the water."

Host a "Come As You Are" party. Send invitations and have
your friends and other couples informally RSVP. The formal
invitation takes place when you show unexpectedly at their
home or work. Whatever they are wearing when you show
up, they must wear later to the party.

Zing . . . zap . . . pow . . . play laser tag.

Organize a group of friends and their dates into a game of baseball, softball, or touch football. Tailgate before and after the game.

Have a theme dinner at home complete with decorations, music, and clothing. Create themes that help you explore and understand other cultures, like Mexican, Chinese, Indian, Caribbean, and more.

Not all paint is for art. Splat . . . splat . . . splat . . . play paint ball with other couples.

Night fever. Night fever. Transport yourselves back to those carefree '70s. Host a disco party complete with strobe lights, tight, flared pants, halter tops, Cheez Whiz, little hot dogs on toothpicks, and of course, funky disco tunes.

Prepare and conduct your own road rally together.
Do it over a weekend and map out where and when you'd like to go.

Develop and create a citywide scavenger hunt.

Get everyone together for *game night*. Play charades or
favorite board games like Scrabble or Monopoly.
Make snacks.

Build a fire, roast some marshmallows, make s'mores, and
tell ghost stories. If you don't know any,
read a scary book out loud.

Don't let the rain get you down. Play a game of mud football
or, for that matter, mud anything.

Have a *BYOL* party.
Bring Your Own Lobster, have a
race, then cook them by how they
finish. Last one to finish gets cooked
first. Oh, poor Larry!

Look for special TV marathons and spend the day watching continuous episodes of *M*A*S*H*, *I Love Lucy*, *Gilligan's Island*, *The Brady Bunch*, *Star Trek*, or *The Real World*.

Play techno hide and seek. Take an hour to hide in an area in the city. Call each other on cellular phones and give hints to your location. One group is mobile or both, you decide. The hiders lead the seekers to the hiding spot through hints alone. Make the final location someplace wonderful to eat.

Why celebrate the stroke of midnight only on New Year's
Eve? Fill a room with balloons, streamers, music, party hats,
and horns and celebrate midnight any night of the year!
Dress up if you like.

Go to a murder mystery play or any theatrical production that
involves the audience. Shows like *Tamara,*
Tony 'N Tina's Wedding, and *The Real Live Brady Bunch* are
always fun.

Host a champagne tasting party!

We just wanted to say:

From John . . . To Mom and Dad, you are my heroes! To Kim, Amy, my entire extended family, Elizabeth D., Adria G., and Cynthia M., thanks for always being there for me. To Andrews and McMeel, and especially Rick Hill, thanks for respecting and taking a group of slackers so seriously. We're excited to have a cool "big brother" like you. And to those people who are busy making this planet a better place, keep it up. We need more positives in the world today. And to buzz boxx, way to go, keep the faith and dreams do come true.

From Stuart . . . I would like to thank my parents for everything. I love you both. To my brothers Lance and Matt, good friends Chappy, Sean and Matt E., Van Gundys, and all those at M. Jacks, may you get a lot of use out of this book! To John for having the faith in me and making this possible. And most importantly to Christine for supporting me, believing in me, putting up with me, understanding me, motivating me, reeling me in, and dragging me to Indy to be run over by my destiny, let's start with page one. I love you.

From Morgan . . . I'd like to thank God, my family, my friends, and all those people who created the Apple Macintosh computer, which made designing this book a whole lot easier.

FRIENDS, ROMANS, COUNTRYMEN, SEND US YOUR DATING IDEAS!

(Or write to us and tell us if you've used one of the ideas from this book or what you think about the book.)

So you think you're a hunka-hunka burnin' love, a love goddess, the brains in your relationship . . . or you just have a cool date idea that you want to share? Our second book is already under way and we'd like to hear from you! Part of what made this book a success was the ideas contributed by a group of people tired of the same old thing and looking for some new date ideas. So if you have an idea that wasn't included in this book, jot it down and send it to us. Please include your name and address in case we want to get hold of you.

Write to us at:

buzz boxx
P.O. Box 40671
Indianapolis, IN 46240-0671

E-mail us at:

buzzboxx@aol.com

Of course if you do submit an idea, you understand that you're willingly sending it to us, you're over 18 years of age, you're releasing all rights to it, you're giving us permission to use it any way we want, including that we may or may not attribute your idea to you by name or use a fictitious name . . . blah, blah, blah. (Our lawyer made us add this . . . are you happy, Dave?)

Thank you.

HEY YOU! THIS IS OUR BLATANT ATTEMPT TO SELL MORE BOOKS!

Did you know that buzz boxx has other books besides this one?
Look for these buzz boxx titles at cooler stores that "get it"
(as in understand the *slacker* set):

1. Pick-Up Lines™: The Best and Worst on Planet Earth